I0155912

A Covid-19 Story For Kids
Why Our Class And The World Cried

Renee Lovekids

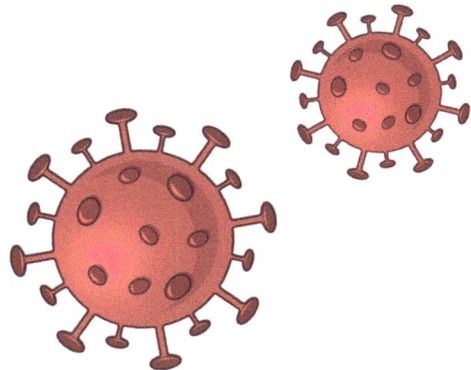

Halo
PUBLISHING
INTERNATIONAL

Copyright © 2021 Renee Lovekids
Illustrated by Chad Thompson
All rights reserved.

No part of this book may be reproduced in any manner
whatsoever without the prior written permission of the publisher,
except in the case of brief quotations embodied in reviews.

ISBN: 978-1-63765-093-6
LCCN: 2021915444

Halo Publishing International, LLC
www.halopublishing.com

Printed and bound in the United States of America

Dedication

to

millions of children affected by COVID 19

to

children and parents I served during the pandemic

to

Mikey & Malachi

And the little boy in Mike and Sam

to

Eugene Jr. and Mildred my biggest fans

to

a world awaiting normalcy

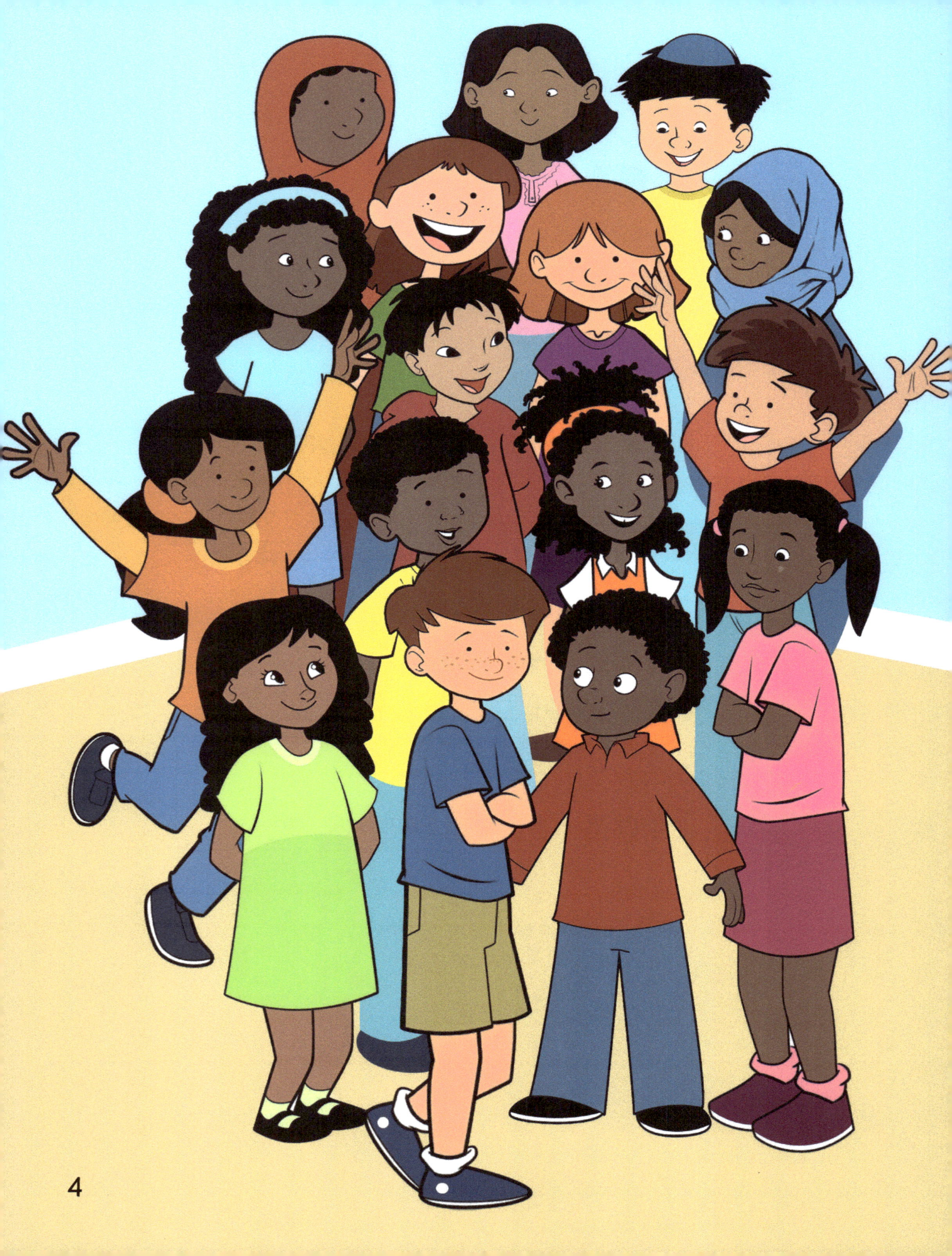

Señora Cruz cried the last time I spoke to you about her. She loved dar tarea (to give homework)! Deberes (homework) is so important to her. This year was no different. Señora Cruz just couldn't get enough of class 4-313. We had such a great year in school. Though her love for homework continued, she made many attempts at transforming the amount of homework she would give. Operative word here is "attempt." Señora Cruz still has not gotten over the class's decision to receive a three-day homework pass instead of a pizza party for winning the "Best Behavior Contest." One day she'll get over it!

Our class had the privilege of having Señora Cruz again this year. As I said, *she couldn't get enough of us*. When a teacher follows or remains with her previous class, it is called "looping." Señora Cruz continued a new year with her former class, with the addition of a few new students. Señora Cruz told our parents that *looping* would prove to be effective because of the relationship she formed with us last year. She understands how we learn along with knowing our strengths, weaknesses and personalities. This would prove to be quite important in the coming months. Many of the routines we had last year were very similar. We continued to have several homework assignments: "Ugh." Señora Cruz still has the "Homework Hall Of Shame" poster for all to see, too: double "Ugh"!

But because our class has a better understanding of how serious Señora Cruz is when it comes to homework, we were a lot more conscious this year about turning in our homework on time. Well, most of us were more intentional about completing those assignments!

When parents and visitors came to our room, we continued to sing, "The Welcome Song." Remember the part of the song that said, "Shake hands no time to be blue," and Señora Cruz would quickly squirt hand sanitizer in the hands of the visitor after we shook their hands? We always wondered why that was so important to her. We joked about her being afraid of germs, but was she right about that? Could our class actually transfer germs to our visitors when we shook their hands? Could they transfer germs to us? Yucky!

Welcome Visitors!

Señora Cruz continued to tell us to "spread love, not germs" if we coughed without covering our mouths with our arms, or not coughing into our shirts. She would repeat that line when someone sneezed and wiped their nose with their hands, and when some children would dig up their nose and touch a chair or desk with that same hand! "Spread love, not germs, class," she would say. She always kept tissues nearby for easy access to protect us from germs. Hand sanitizers were always kept nearby, too!

One day when Señora Cruz fussed at Jerome for not covering his mouth when he coughed, Malachi asked her to tell us more about germs and how they spread to others. Señora Cruz looked serious and began to explain.

Germs appear to be invisible but they are tiny, tiny organisms and can be seen under a microscope. Because we can't see them, we don't realize we have them and carry them. Germs are really easy to spread!" she said. So, that's why Señora Cruz says, "Spread love, not germs," I thought to myself as Señora Cruz continued the lesson. She said germs are also called microbes. They all travel together like an army and can form into viruses. "Viruses?" asked Ali. Yes, viruses! They can be found anywhere and everywhere! Some germs can make us sick. When they get into your body, they can multiply, causing you to become ill. They can cause diseases.

Vivienne, who's really smart when it comes to art and science, kindly interrupted, and asked, "Is that why you squirt the hand sanitizer in the visitor's hands after our song?"

"Great question, Vivienne, and yes, that is why I do it! So often we will cough and sneeze into our hands without thinking and then touch someone or something.

"If we wipe our noses with our hands and then wipe them on our shirts or pants, won't that take away the germs?" Mikey asked.

"It may get rid of some of the germs, but not all. Soap and water or sanitizer are the best ways to clean your hands.

Germs or Microbes: Tiny organism that can cause diseases. They can enter the body through the nose, mouth or an open wound like a scratch or sore

Bacteria: Living cells. They can be good for you or bad. The good bacteria help you digest food. They can be found in some foods and soil. The bad bacteria make you sick and can cause infection.

Virus: Microorganisms: They can cause disease; they are smaller than bacteria and can invade our bodies through the nose, mouth or an open wound like a scratch or sore.

Disease: A change in a living body (person or plant) that prevents it from functioning normally; sickness.

Hand hygiene: the procedure of cleansing hands thoroughly using soap and warm water, rubbing hands together for 15 seconds to remove dirt, grime or germs, rinsing hands, and drying hands.

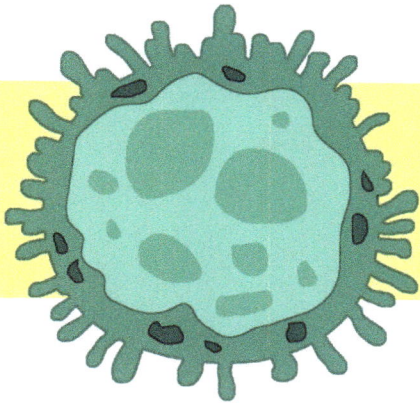

Germ

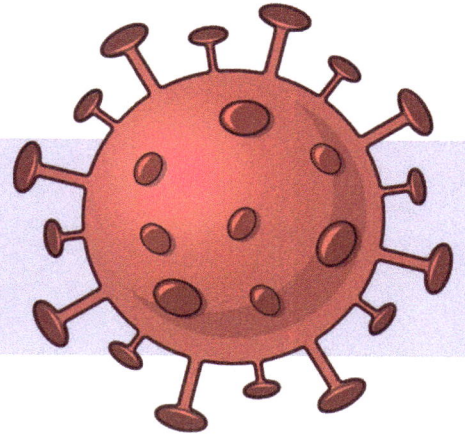

Virus

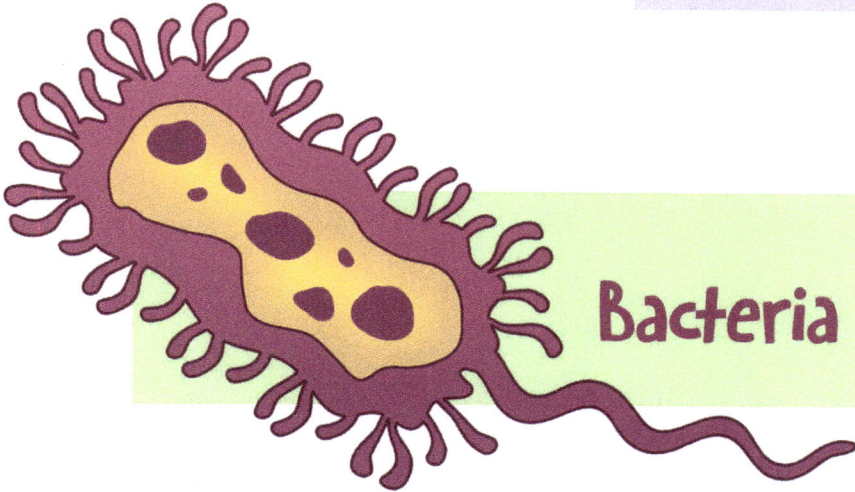

Bacteria

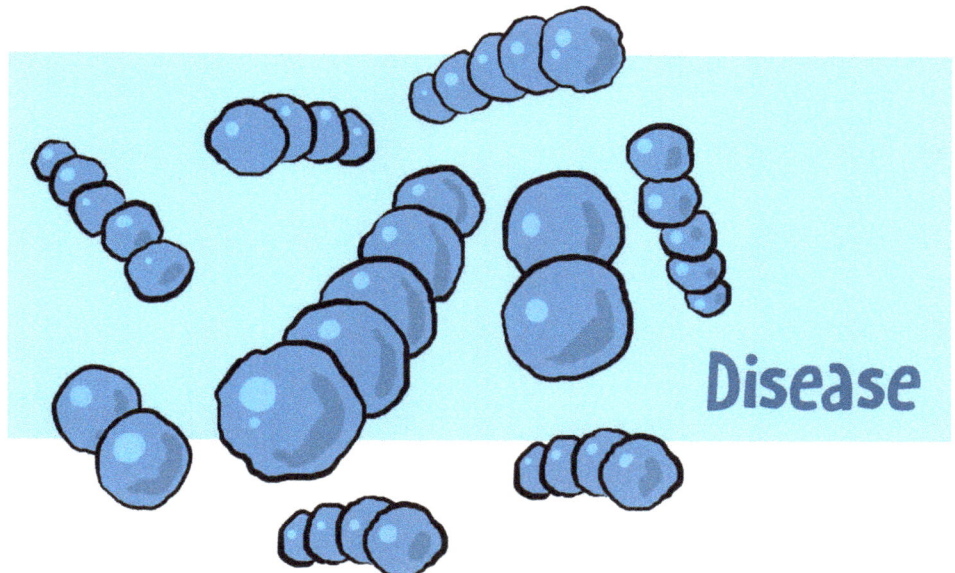

Disease

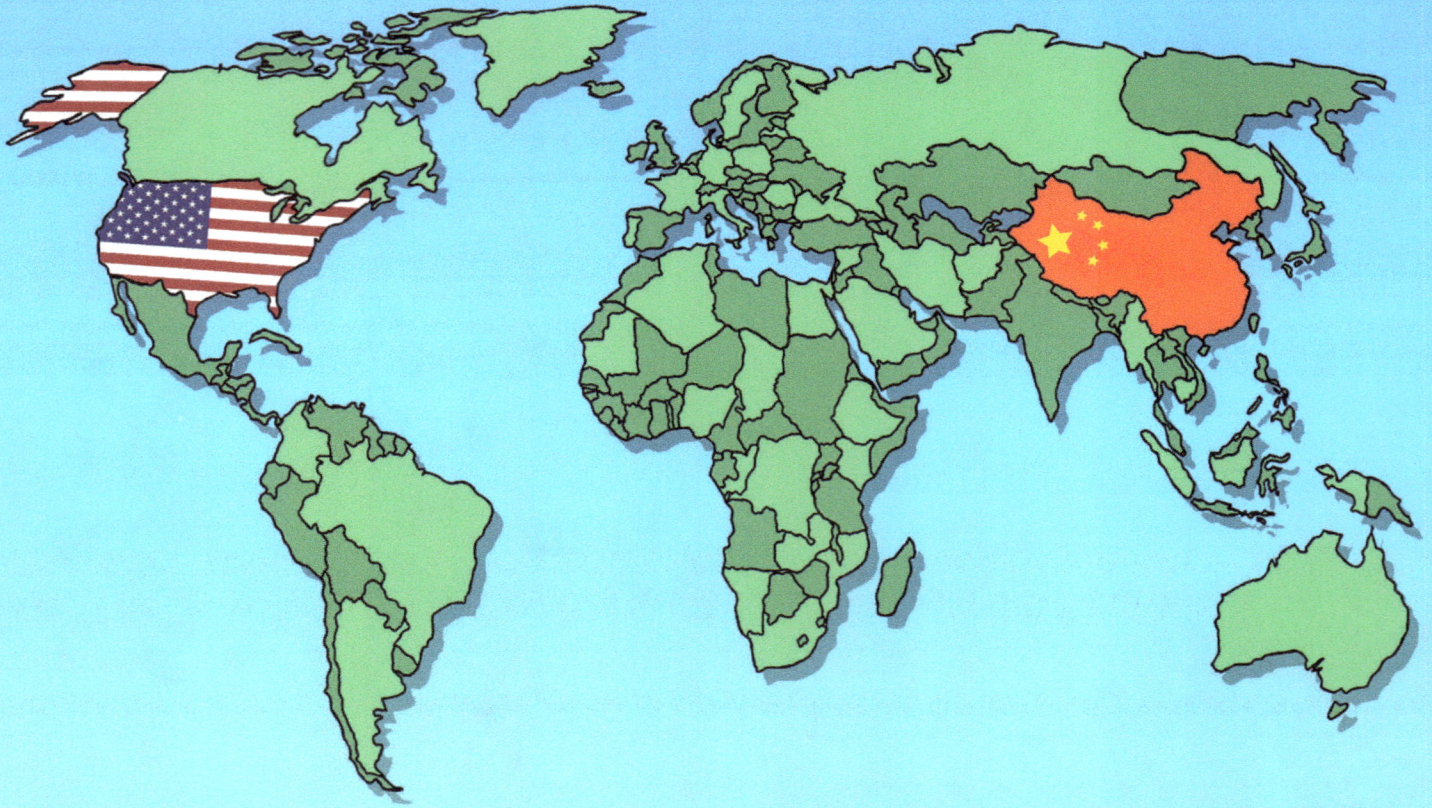

Months later in February, I remember hearing on the news about a virus in China. I wasn't sure how serious it was and hoped it wouldn't come to the United States. Weeks after hearing that report, I saw a few people at the mall wearing masks. It also occurred to me that Señora Cruz began to have more discussions in class about germs and hand hygiene.

Was the disease now in the United States, I asked myself? As my dad and I rode the 7 train, I asked my dad why some of the passengers were wearing mask and he said they were protecting themselves from the coronavirus in case it came to New York. As I walked to school, I saw a few more people wearing them, too! It appeared so strange to me. I wondered if I would have to cover my mouth and nose, too. It looked a little scary and uncomfortable.

Amaya and Amira, who are really smart and observant, said they noticed how our teacher was behaving too. Every morning since then, we observed Señora Cruz cleaning everything in sight! She cleansed colored markers, our classroom sink, the door and door knobs. Why is she doing this, I thought. She continued wiping down the computers, Smart Board, laptops, chairs and book baskets. Malachi whispered, "We should stay out of her way before she starts washing us!"

Daily, as the class entered the room in the morning, it smelled fresh and sanitized. Señora Cruz always kept our classroom clean in the past, but not like this! My classmates began to hear more about the corona virus on the evening news. Teachers were talking about it quietly to each other! They were cleaning and sanitizing their rooms to keep their students safe as well! We noticed that our classmates began missing class. They were out sick. Many complained of coughing and fever and some had tummy problems. Had that scary disease come to New York and to our school?

We all noticed that Señora Cruz kept our classroom windows cracked wider, even though it was cold outside.

The class started talking more about the disease. Our parents sent us to school with sanitizers! Zhyla's daddy made a special mixture of sanitizer and aloe for her. It was a bluish-green color! She shared her dad's formula with her friends Isabella, Kelsey, Angelo (who said he was going to ask his dad to create a formula), Malachi and Aaron. They sat at Zhyla's table.

Señora Cruz kept reminding us to use our own tools and supplies. She asked us not to borrow from each other anymore. The class resumed putting our coats and backpacks in a large plastic bag to separate our personal belongings, which we hung in the coat closet. This all happened as we were celebrating Black History Month and beginning Women's History Month. We were involved in fun activities and projects and it helped us keep our minds off of what was happening in our state of New York, the United States, and the world.

I remember our class celebrating the life of legendary NBA player Kobe Bryant during Black History Month. We created a wall display for Kobe and hanger projects for other influential African Americans.

Next, our class began a study of women through songs and videos of women such as Sonia Sotomayor, First Lady Michelle Obama, Susan B. Anthony, Ruth Bader Ginsburg, Harriet Tubman, Hillary Clinton, Malala Yousafzai, Katherine Johnson and other courageous women. We did research in groups, sharing ideas and using the internet together. These projects really comforted us concerning some of the tension that was building in our school and our city now that COVID-19 had arrived in New York. On Thursday and Friday, (March 12 and 13, 2020), Señora Cruz began asking the class to place their textbooks in large containers she purchased from Ikea. Each table group had one. We were keeping less on our desks. I think it was to keep our personal areas safe. Little did we know that March 13, 2020 would be our last day in school. It was the last day we would be together in our classroom.

School closings...

SPREAD LOVE, NOT GERMS

On March 15th, an announcement was made on the evening news and our mayor declared that the schools were closed.

I don't think parents and teachers were surprised, but I know that I was and so were my classmates. Once our school closed, and hearing all the news about COVID-19, I was so grateful that Señora Cruz took spreading germs seriously and warned us about it! Now all we hear from our parents and commercials is to keep our hands washed and cleansed regularly during the day! I am so happy that she had sanitizers in different places in our classroom and tissue boxes, too! Señora Cruz instructed every class she ever taught her motto: "Spread love, not germs!" It may have prevented many of us from catching this awful virus!

Things changed for my classmates and me! Everything about school and being in a classroom changed for the whole world! I bet every kid on the plant wondered if school life would get back to normal. I have to admit it was kind of fun being home, but after a month or two I really began to miss my classmates and Señora Cruz. No more competing with other groups and getting points for participation or good grades. No more of Señora Cruz acting silly, making faces or making us laugh. No more gym, dance, art, music or technology.

Now, the whole world is crying for their families who became sick from the virus, or worse. The world is waiting for things to return to normal and for other things to change!

So many things have happened since COVID-19 entered our nation and world! Stores were closed, in addition to restaurants, gyms, stadiums, recreational places, barber shops, etc.

The world was now introduced to a strange term: "Remote Learning." It proved to be a challenge for teachers, parents and children. Señora Cruz wasn't aware how long schools would be closed, so she didn't take many teacher manuals and books home to use. It took a while for Señora Cruz and our class to adjust to using technology and Google classroom. She initially had difficulty teaching and using the technology, but as she became more familiar with it, she was able to laugh a little more! We had many challenges to overcome, such as internet issues, and educational programs that we were sometimes unable to access on certain servers. My parents were frustrated, too, because there are three kids in my family. I remember some families whose first language was not English struggled too! Our school was able to provide devices for students.

Yet, with all the confusion, our teacher found ways to make learning fun. She made videos to teach reading, writing and math. They were informative and some were really funny. We created science experiments together, too! She was even able to email gift certificates from Dunkin Donuts to students that participated and were productive. We did eventually resume music, dance, gym, art and technology classes! Yay! Señora Cruz said that the parents were the real heroes of "Remote Learning." She said we were too! She got us through this scary time that made my class and the world cry. I really hope this pandemic ends soon!

www.ingramcontent.com/pod-product-compliance
Lightning Source LLC
Chambersburg PA
CBHW060902090426
42738CB00025B/3497